Why do flowers like bees?

camilla de la Bedoyere

First published in 2012 by Miles Kelly Publishing Ltd
Harding's Barn, Bardfield End Green, Thaxted,
Essex, CM6 3PX, UK

2 4 6 8 10 9 7 5 3 1

Publishing Director Belinda Gallagher
Creative Director Jo Cowan
Volume Design Redmoor Design, Kayleigh Allen
Cover Designer Kayleigh Allen
Image Manager Liberty Newton
Indexer Jane Parker
Production Manager Elizabeth Collins
Reprographics Stephan Davis, Anthony Cambray

ISBN 978-1-84810-617-8

Printed in China

British Library Cataloguing-in-Publication Data

A catalogue record for this book is
available from the British Library

ACKNOWLEDGEMENTS
The publishers would like to thank the following
artists who have contributed to this book:

Mike Foster (character cartoons)

All other artwork from the Miles Kelly Artwork Bank

The publishers would like to thank the following
sources for the use of their photographs:

FLPA 28 Wayne Hutchinson
Fotolia 24 Giovanni Catalani
Shutterstock.com Front cover Andrey Snegirev;
5 satit_srihin; 7 Anest; 8 urosr; 10 artjazz; 12 Nazzu;
15 nagib; 17 kkaplin; 18 Cathy Keifer; 21 NatalieJean;
27 Vishnevskiy Vasily; 29 Shi Yali

All other photographs are from:
Corel, digitalSTOCK, digitalvision, John Foxx, PhotoAlto,
PhotoDisc, PhotoEssentials, PhotoPro, Stockbyte

Every effort has been made to acknowledge the
source and copyright holder of each picture.
Miles Kelly Publishing apologises for any
unintentional errors or omissions.

Made with paper from a sustainable forest

www.mileskelly.net
info@mileskelly.net

www.factsforprojects.com

contents

what is a plant? 4

Do bananas grow on trees? 5

Did dinosaurs eat plants? 5

why do flowers like bees? 6

can plants move? 7

who knocks nuts? 7

How tall can a tree grow? 8

why do hummingbirds hum? 9

can plants live in a desert? 9

why do flowers smell nice? 10

which plants can pop? 11

Do toads sit on toadstools? 11

what is an upside-down tree? 12

why don't plants fall over? 13

which bird pretends to be
a tree? 13

Can plants grow on animals? 14

why are leaves green? 15

why do otters sleep in
seaweed? 15

why do moths need long
tongues? 16

what is the biggest flower? 17

Do plants have eyes? 17

why are some plants sticky? 18

why do bluebells grow in spring? 19

Does spaghetti grow on trees? 19

How do ants protect trees? 20

Can plants live underwater? 21

where does paper come from? 21

why do lizards lick flowers? 22

who lives in a tree house? 23

Do needles grow on trees? 23

why do leaves turn red? 24

How do seeds grow? 25

which tree can you drink from? 25

why do plants have teeth? 26

What happens underground? 27

How do birds help plants? 27

which seeds can hitch a ride? 28

can grass grow as tall as
trees? 29

what is a rainforest? 29

Quiz 30

Index 32

what is a plant?

Bud

Flower

A plant is a living thing that breathes, grows and changes. Plants live all over the world, even in deserts, on mountains and underwater. Most plants have flowers, leaves, stems and roots.

Leaf

Stem

Roots

Do bananas grow on trees?

No, but bananas do grow on plants that are almost as tall as trees. A banana plant has one main stem and one big flower. A single bunch of bananas grows from the flower.

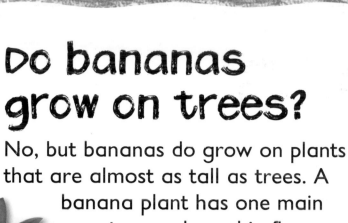

Bananas

Potato bug

Big animals eat plants, but so do little ones! Bugs, slugs and mini-beasts all enjoy nibbling fruits, shoots, roots and leaves.

Make

Ask a grown up to help you make a milkshake. You need ice cream, bananas and milk.

Did dinosaurs eat plants?

Some dinosaurs feasted on meat, but the biggest ones munched on plants. They probably spent all day eating to get enough energy for their giant bodies to keep moving!

Why do flowers like bees?

Bee collecting pollen

Flowers like bees, and bees like flowers! Bees help flowers to grow seeds, and flowers give bees food. Look at a flower and you will see a yellow dust, called pollen. Bees eat pollen, and collect it to take back to their hives.

Seedlings

can plants move?

Plants don't have arms, legs or wings, but they can still move. All plants need sunlight, and they can bend their stems so their leaves face the Sun.

Grow

Grow some cress seedlings. Look at how the seedlings bend towards the light as they grow.

Pollen coat

Bats are flying animals that come out at night. They feed on flower nectar and can get covered in pollen!

who knocks nuts?

Birds called nutcrackers do! Nuts are seeds with hard shells. Nutcrackers open nuts by bashing them against rocks. The hard shells fall away, and the bird can eat the seed inside.

How tall can a tree grow?

The tallest trees in the world are called giant redwoods. Some redwoods are more than 100 metres tall – that's enormous! These trees don't just grow tall, they grow old too. A redwood tree can live for 2000 years, or more.

← Giant redwood tree

Plant

Plant two bean seeds in different pots. Only water one pot. Which seed grows?

why do hummingbirds hum?

Tiny hummingbirds beat their wings so fast, they make a humming sound. These birds also hover — when they beat their wings they stay in one place. This means they can drink nectar from a flower without having to land on it.

sweet smell

Rose petals have a lovely scent. Long ago, ladies put petals in their bath water to make it smell lovely.

Cacti

can plants live in a desert?

Yes they can. Plants need water to live, but it doesn't often rain in a desert. Cacti are plants that live in very dry places, and they have tiny spiny leaves. When it rains, cacti save water in their fat stems.

Why do flowers smell nice?

Flowers smell nice because they want animals to visit them. When a butterfly feeds on a flower's nectar, it picks up pollen on its feet and takes it to another flower. There, the pollen joins with an egg, and grows into a seed.

Butterfly feeding on nectar

which plants can pop?

Squirting cucumbers can squirt their seeds 5 metres away! Their seedpods are full of water, and pop when they are ripe, sending their brown seeds far and wide.

Make

Ask a grown up to make popcorn wth you. When the air inside each piece of corn gets hot, it pops!

Do toads sit on toadstools?

Hungry bugs

Caterpillars spend all day eating leaves and growing. They are so hungry that one caterpillar can eat every leaf on a plant.

Toads sometimes sit on toadstools, but they prefer to hide in the damp grass and leaves underneath them. Toadstools and mushrooms are types of fungus. Some fungi are very poisonous.

Toadstools and mushrooms

what is an upside-down tree?

Baobab trees are called upside-down trees. They have big, fat trunks and stumpy little branches that look like roots, especially when their leaves have fallen off. These funny-looking trees grow in Africa.

Baobab trees

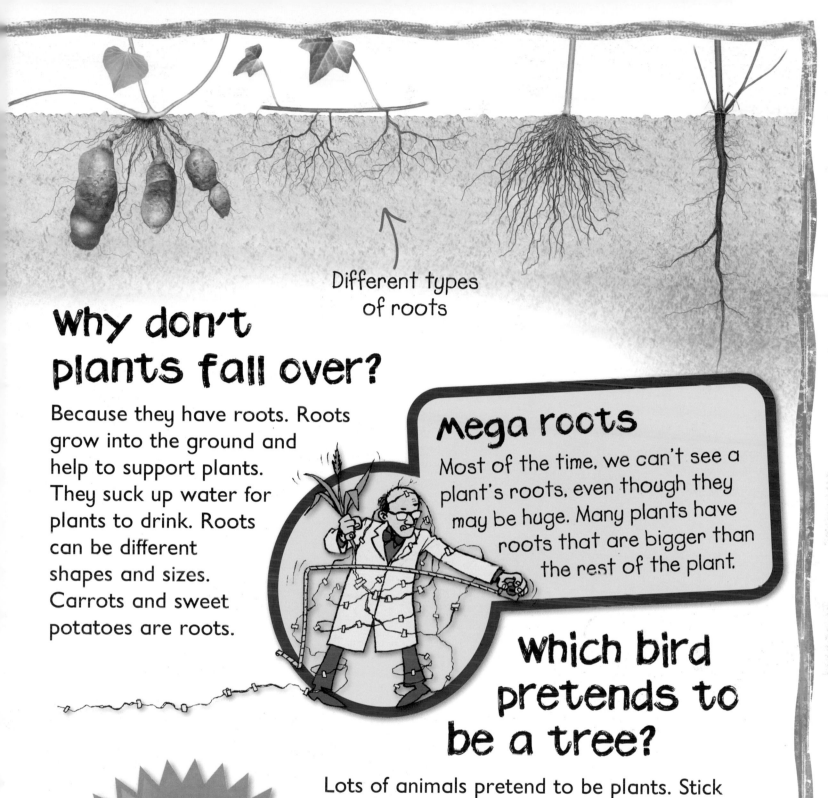

Different types of roots

Why don't plants fall over?

Because they have roots. Roots grow into the ground and help to support plants. They suck up water for plants to drink. Roots can be different shapes and sizes. Carrots and sweet potatoes are roots.

mega roots

Most of the time, we can't see a plant's roots, even though they may be huge. Many plants have roots that are bigger than the rest of the plant.

which bird pretends to be a tree?

Lots of animals pretend to be plants. Stick insects pretend to be twigs, leaf bugs look like leaves, and potoos are birds that pretend to be dead branches. It's a very good disguise!

Draw

Draw a butterfly feeding on a flower. Use bright paints, crayons or pens to colour it in.

can plants grow on animals?

It's strange to think of plants growing on animals, but it is possible. Sloths live in the jungle. They move so slowly that tiny plants, called algae, grow in their fur. It makes the sloths look green!

Mother and baby sloths

Why are leaves green?

Leaves are green because they are filled with a special green substance, which helps plants to make their food. All plants need sunlight, air and water to make food.

Green leaves

Sun fun

Plants can only make food during the day, when the sun shines. At night they rest, just like we do.

Find

Collect leaves that have different shapes and use them to make some leaf prints. You will need paper and paint.

Why do otters sleep in seaweed?

Sea otters wrap strands of seaweed around themselves so they don't float away. They like to sleep and eat wrapped up like this.

Why do moths need long tongues?

Moths and butterflies need long tongues to reach the nectar deep inside a flower. Nectar is a sugary juice that lots of insects and birds like to drink. It tastes sweet, and it gives them lots of energy too.

Tongue

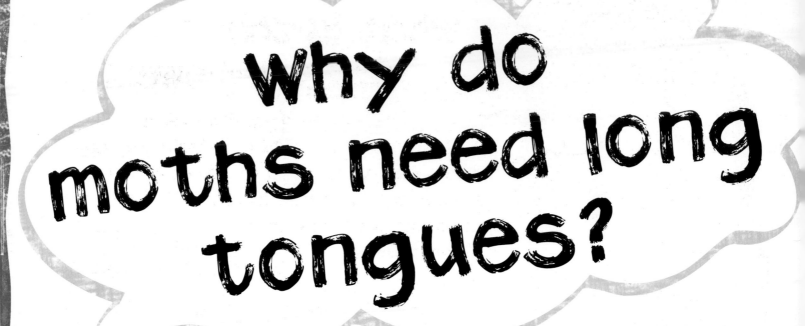

Moth feeding on nectar

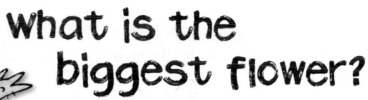

What is the biggest flower?

The world's biggest flower is enormous. It is called a rafflesia, and one bloom can measure up to 100 centimetres wide. Rafflesia flowers have five petals and they grow in rainforests.

Go away!

The spines on a cactus are sharp, little leaves. Plants stop animals from eating them with thorns, spines and even nasty tastes.

Rafflesia flower

Do plants have eyes?

Plants don't have eyes and they cannot see. Sometimes we say that potatoes have 'eyes', but these are just the places where roots and stems are starting to grow.

Measure

Use a measuring tape to see how big a rafflesia is. Is it bigger than you?

why are some plants sticky?

Sundew plants are sticky so they can catch flies. When a fly lands on the drops of sugary juice, it soon discovers that its feet are stuck to the plant. Sundew plants catch flies because they like to eat them!

Fly →

Sundew plant

Bluebell plant

why do bluebells grow in spring?

Most plants rest in winter and come to life again in spring. Bluebells, daffodils and tulips all grow in the early spring. They appear as soon as the days begin to get longer, and before trees grow new leaves.

Make!

Ask a grown up to help you make a fruit salad using lots of different fruits.

Fire starter

Fires don't just kill plants, they can help them grow. The seeds from giant redwood trees only start to grow after there has been a forest fire.

Does spaghetti grow on trees?

No, but it does come from a plant. Spaghetti and bread are made from wheat, which is a plant that grows in almost every country of the world.

HOW do ants protect trees?

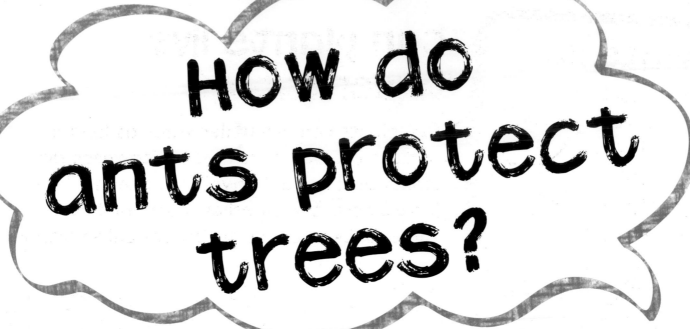

Ants protect trees by biting animals that try to eat the leaves. In Africa, cows like to eat acacia trees, where ants live and build their nests. When a cow tries to nibble the tasty leaves, the ants run over and bite it!

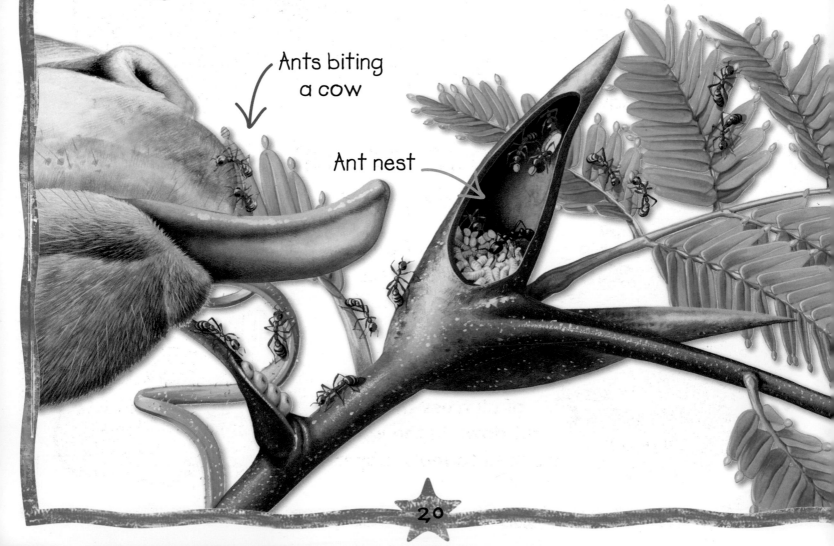

Ants biting a cow

Ant nest

20

Shake it!

Some plants have smart ways to stay alive. If there has not been enough rain, quiver trees drop entire branches.

can plants live underwater?

Yes, plants can live underwater as long as sunlight can still reach them. Seaweeds are plants that live underwater in oceans. They look different from other plants and have thick rubbery leaves, which are called fronds.

Seaweed

where does paper come from?

Bake

Flour comes from a plant called wheat. Bake some biscuits, bread or cakes using flour.

Paper comes from trees. When trees are cut down to make paper, many animals lose their homes. Nearly half of all trees that are cut down in the world are used to make paper.

why do lizards lick flowers?

Most lizards eat bugs, but some of them feed on flowers. This blue-tailed day lizard licks a flower to reach the nectar inside. By doing this, the lizard also helps to transfer pollen to other flowers.

Blue-tailed day lizard →

who lives in a tree house?

Some people who live in rainforests live in tree houses. They build their homes at the top of trees. Tree houses keep people safe from their enemies, and from deadly animals.

super grass

Billions of animals eat grass. They are called grazing animals. Sheep, horses, zebras and rabbits are grazing animals.

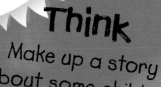

Think

Make up a story about some children who live in a tree house.

Do needles grow on trees?

Yes they do! The long, thin leaves that grow on pine trees are called needles. Pine trees live in cold places, and their seeds grow in cones. Most trees lose leaves in autumn, but pine trees keep theirs all year.

Pine cone

Pine needles

why do leaves turn red?

At the end of the summer, leaves begin to die. As they die, their colours turn from green to red, gold and brown, before they fall from the tree. This time is called autumn. During winter, the trees will rest, but they are still alive.

Trees in autumn

HOW do seeds grow?

When the time is right, seeds begin to grow into new plants. They need water, air and warmth to grow. First, a small, white root grows. Then, a new green shoot grows up to the light. Soon, new green leaves grow too.

Leaves

Seed

Green shoot

Find

Go on a nature hunt in autumn. Ask a grown up to help you find colourful leaves, berries, conkers and acorns.

Brrrrrr!

Trees and plants don't feel the cold, like we do, but very frosty weather can kill plants.

which tree can you drink from?

In remote places in Australia, native people drink from the paperbark tree if water is scarce. The trunk is full of sweet liquid that is safe to drink.

25

Why do plants have teeth?

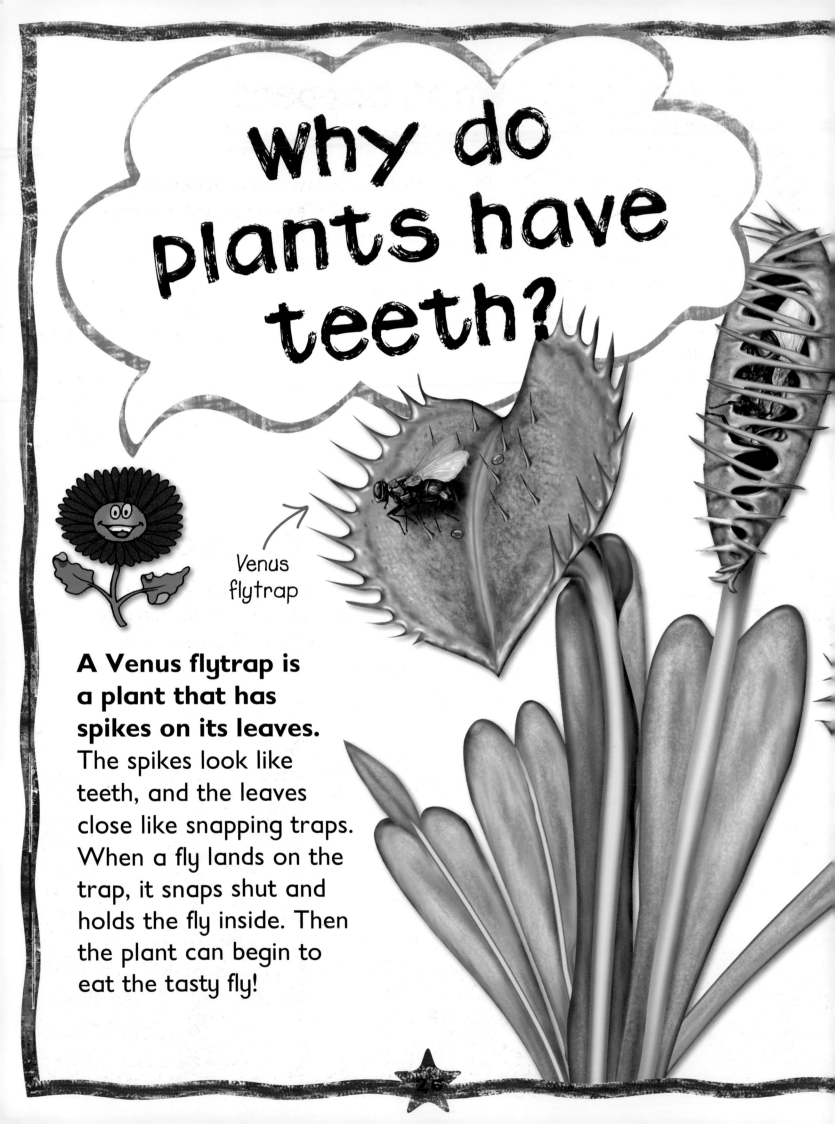

Venus flytrap

A Venus flytrap is a plant that has spikes on its leaves. The spikes look like teeth, and the leaves close like snapping traps. When a fly lands on the trap, it snaps shut and holds the fly inside. Then the plant can begin to eat the tasty fly!

Fussy koalas

Koalas only eat leaves from gum trees. They spend up to 22 hours every day fast asleep, and eat for the rest of the time.

What happens underground?

Plants grow in soil, which is full of tiny animals. Some of these bugs and worms eat roots, but most of them help to make the soil a healthy place for plants.

How do birds help plants?

Birds eat berries and fruits from plants. When a bird eats a fruit, the seed inside passes through its body and comes out in its poo. This seed may grow into a new plant.

Dig

Ask a grown up to choose a plant to dig up. Can you find any bugs in the soil around the roots?

Bird eating berries

Which seeds can hitch a ride?

Seeds with prickles can hitch a ride. Grazing animals often walk through plants that have prickly seeds. The prickles can hook onto the animal's fur. The seeds fall off later, and may grow into new plants.

Prickly seed

Sheep with prickles in its fur

can grass grow as tall as trees?

Bamboo is a type of grass. It grows very fast – up to 30 centimetres in just one day! In Asia, there are bamboo forests where each plant grows as tall as a tree. Bamboo stems are hollow, and they can bend in the wind without breaking.

Healthy veg

We need to eat plants to be healthy. Fruit and vegetables are full of vitamins, which help us to grow and stay well.

Bamboo forest

what is a rainforest?

Rainforests are big, thick forests that grow in hot places. It rains almost every day in a rainforest. These forests are special because so many different types of animals and plants live in them.

Measure

If a plant grows 10 centimetres in one day, how much will it grow in one week?

Quiz time

Do you remember what you have read about plant life? Here are some questions to test your memory. The pictures will help you. If you get stuck, read the pages again.

page 9

3. Can plants live in a desert?

page 11

4. Which plants can pop?

page 5

1. Did dinosaurs eat plants?

5. Why do otters sleep in seaweed?

page 15

2. Why do flowers like bees?

6. Why do moths need long tongues?

page 16

page 6

7. Do plants have eyes?

page 17

11. Who lives in a tree house?

page 23

page 25

8. Why do bluebells grow in spring?

page 19

12. Which tree can you drink from?

13. How do birds help plants?

page 27

9. Where does paper come from?

page 21

10. Why do lizards lick flowers?

page 22

Answers

1. Yes, lots of dinosaurs ate plants
2. Because bees help flowers to grow seeds
3. Yes, cacti are plants that live in deserts
4. Squirting cucumbers pop
5. To stop themselves floating away
6. To reach nectar deep inside flowers
7. No, but potatoes have places called 'eyes' where roots and stems start to grow
8. Because the days begin to grow longer
9. Paper comes from trees
10. To eat the nectar inside
11. Some rainforest people live in tree houses
12. The paperbark tree
13. By eating berries and fruits, birds can help new plants to spread and grow

Index

A

acacia trees 20
acorns 25
air 15, 25
algae 14
ants 20
autumn 23, 24, 25

B

bamboo 29
bananas 5
baobab trees 12
bats 7
bees 6
berries 25, 27
birds 7, 9, 13, 27
blue-tailed day
    lizard 22
bluebells 19
bugs 5, 13, 27
butterflies 10, 13,
    16

C

cacti 9, 17
carrots 13
caterpillars 11
cones 23
conkers 25

D, E

daffodils 19
deserts 4, 9
dinosaurs 5
disguise 13
eggs 10
energy 5, 16

F

fire 19
flour 21
flowers 4, 5, 6, 7, 9,
    10, 16, 17, 22
fronds 21
fruits 5, 19, 27, 29
fungi 11

G

giant redwood
    trees 8, 19
grass 23, 29
grazing animals 23,
    28
gum trees 27

H, J, K

hummingbirds 9
jungles 14
koalas 27

L

leaves 4, 5, 7, 9, 11,
    15, 17, 20, 21,
    23, 24, 25, 26
light 7, 25
lizards 22

M

mini-beasts 5
moths 16

mushrooms 11

N, O

nectar 7, 9, 10, 16,
    22
needles 23
nutcrackers 7
nuts 7
otters 15

P

paper 21
petals 9, 17
pine cones 23
pine needles 23
pollen 6, 7, 10, 22
potatoes 17
potoos 13
prickles 28

Q, R

quiver trees 21
rafflesia flower 17
rainforests 17, 23,
    29
redwoods 8, 19
roots 4, 5, 13, 17,
    25, 27
rose petals 9

S

scent (smell) 9, 10
sea otters 15
seaweed 15, 21
seedlings 7
seedpods 11
seeds 6, 7, 10, 11,
    19, 23, 25, 27, 28
shoots 5, 25
sloths 14

slugs 5
soil 27
spines 9, 17
spring 19
squirting cucumbers
    11
stems 4, 5, 7, 9, 17,
    29
stick insects 13
summer 24
sundew plants 18
sunlight 7, 15, 21
sweet potatoes 13

T

tastes 17
thorns 17
toads 11
toadstools 11
tree houses 23
trees 5, 8, 12, 20,
    21, 24, 25
trunks 12
tulips 19

U, V

underwater plants
    21
vegetables 29
Venus flytraps 26
vitamins 29

W

warmth 25
water 4, 9, 13, 15,
    25
wheat 19, 21
winter 19, 24
wood 21
worms 27